Eurochants

Also by Adrian Clarke

Imperfect Copies (Bran's Head Press, 1981)
Reading Reverdy (Actual Size, 1985)
Ghost Measures (Actual Size)
Shadow Sector (Writers Forum, 1988)
Spectral Investments (Writers Forum, 1991)
Obscure Disasters (Writers Forum, 1993)
Doing the Thing (Writers Forum, 1997)
Automatic (Mainstream, 1998)
Millennial Shades & Three Papers (Writers Forum, 1998)
Five Doubles & a Chaser (Writers Forum, 1999)
Paradise Gardens (Writers Forum, 2000)
Phantom Returns (Writers Forum, 2001)
Skeleton Sonnets (Writers Forum, 2002)
Former Haunts (Veer Books, 2004)
Possession (Veer Books, 2007)

Eurochants

Adrian Clarke

Shearsman Books
Exeter

First published in the United Kingdom in 2010 by
Shearsman Books Ltd
58 Velwell Road
Exeter EX4 4LD

www.shearsman.com

ISBN 978-1-84861-095-8
First Edition

Copyright © Adrian Clarke, 2010.

The right of Adrian Clarke to be identified as the author of this work has been asserted by him in accordance with the Copyrights, Designs and Patents Act of 1988.
All rights reserved.

Acknowledgements
Thanks to the editors of *Great Works*, *Oasis*, *onedit*, *Poetry Salzburg Review*, *Veer Away* and *Veer Off* in which versions of some of these poems first appeared.

Contents

Chinese Whispers 7

Seconds
Satire 1 19
From the Annals 23
Preamble to a Legacy 28
NW1 After-Image 31

Reading Max Jacob
1914 35
War 36
Declamatory Poem 37
Poem 38
Christmas Story 39
Cubism and Sun Diluted 40
Literary Manners 41
Journeys 42
1889–1916 43
In the Silent Forest 44
Kaleidoscope 45
We Saw It But It's Impossible 46
For M. Modigliani to Show Him I Am a Poet 47
Villonelle 48
Madame X 49
Cemetery 50
The Acrobat in Third Class 51
Do You Know Meister Eckhart? 52
Wars and America 53
Love of One's Neighbour 54

Eurochants
    I   57
    II   71
    III   85

Terminal Preludes   99

Chinese Whispers

regional ineffable
knelt before
bequest assemblies
generate lots
of god's
own
    Oedipal
I'n't it ?
Thyestian banquet
vide THEMIS
blood ties
lunate flag
wavers lay
claim to
a community
of states
Zhongguo logo
flown in
with wild
ducks
    elixir
a fifth
unfleshed element
lineage at
swim with
strange fish

Daybreak branches
particles scattering
the red
light maps
a curious
feel time
past deletes
parts she
scintillates through
the film
of script
frost grips
a figure
you can
whistle drawing
the stopped
process call
it a
whirlwind events
occur once
standing there
different factors
holding the
remnants together

pure air
beyond our
last gasp
token ardour's
lunged edge
whittled willowy
peaching below
abdomen switch
width patent
studs tight
laced in
extension slight
delivered through
further exposures
wind chimes
with links
a low
moan's consonance
submission bench
marks liquidity
a rigour
tow path
genitives' dead
lettered release

a stale
breath steps
back shadows
sough Out
Of Nowhere
opposed to
the lyric
drift lingers
still vocal
in person
less static
than moot
ultimate
        after
the fact
yew tree
digits late
history scrolls
down
        woebegone
in memoriam
their fractions
my feelings
refrain to
echo from
the record

separation in
duplicate off
peak clouds
a journey
between whispers
changed times
continue pre
dawn attachment
on the
rack of
dollar value
rising pavements
retraced where
another's steps
stamped out
a might
have gone
begging in
wine fumes
lingers to
the last
crust of
a shared
not ever

an ill
wind flickering
lashes 19
17 gypsy
and griot
gaps in
the Annals
exotic steps
fill half
masked flaring
miscegenist alae
moonlight eclipsed
a hollow
ring's fluted
silver scales
the limits
distant in
the mix
tinkling fringed
Silk Road
declivities full
tilt to
Paris in
spavined ragtime

cold air
the long
nights from
a distance
moon at
the full
a diphthong
the letter
that renames
it short
or imperfect
a forgetting
endemic mirror
a limbo
thirty years
apart *Lune*
nulle not
one smeared
at speed
words on
the further
shore a
different hand
crossed out

aspirant the
kalashnikov lotus
mounted flesh
relic equipage
a parchment
scarred icon
willows systolic
flagellants log
no Boat
That's Leaving
foliage knee
deep through
sagittal latitudes
terminal rebrands
the body
electric virtuality
a ripe
fruit end
user free
access location
apart opulence
means nothing
Out of
This World

Seconds

SATIRE 1

> *ten cirratorum centum dictata fuisse*
> *pro nihilo pendes?*
>   Persius

Apostrophized matters. Cool about mug
shots?—Decipherment a conceptual zilch.
Twice over <u>precisely</u> a self
defeating clique. Personal cracks the
oligochrome Logueistics; "Go easy on
figments" rushing a judgemental double
edge. Blanked out with logorrhoeic
Cambridge blockheads checks the brick
bats that flatter creative lack.
Rife at all stages. Self
ultimacy PERIOD Root out ageism
with the long on the
truth. Stamina jacks up bed
sit iambics; likewise the asthmatic
bar room breath line. Xmas
an assembled public of 6.
Eye contact strains to make
the top shelf bracket: subscriptive
offspring sat pretty on a
clitoral itch. With mobile; unmoved.
Short shrift for PATRONS ARE
REQUESTED. The real stuff on
tap, cut up plasmic gutturals
flop. Adverted, Viagra go hang.
Dissemination withers on the tree.
Spare me the Brecht: parallel
text singularities beg "almost a
crime". Sweet smell listed, alphabet
free: a hundred *that's him*s

in cyberspace evidence no joke.
Ditto the recorded Laureate's voice:
"... the bronze of immortal poesy".
—Heritage culture with a morbid
tinge. Psychics foresee free seats
for the elite; outstripped, happy
the poet's ashes: "Ballerinas too
early for music", the cracked
slab pushes up daffs. Don't
sniff at injustice so fast:
this stuff gets lisped by
kids. Interlocutory textual neurosis. Simultaneously
classics and recycled chip wrappings
on the nail. In this
age, I mean what you
pay. Endorse that fat cheque
with Prize dicks' squeals of
"Exquisite"; save "value" for real
estate. Security's paramount. Shoot
the messenger (forget Pope's dues):
hexameters to Xbox, Homer was
too right. Segue to elegiacs,
a medicinal shot empowers privileged
misery to tell it like
it is. Prosthetics and distended
bellies tippexed, pig yourself on
the lexicon of a globe
trotting opulence. Back home, tills
tell the plain truth: sell
out or zip up. Janus
faced, eyes in your arse
hit the epithet that counts.
Forward means a bid for
"the imaginative franchise". Improve, not
"improv". When did competition rule

out work on the line?
Ditch the semantics, meritocrats care:
ascendancy discards superior crusts. Enduringly,
an epic "yes" to piss
"Sizzling in our . . . grassy language".
"Vowels ploughed"; "green fields greying";
the "verb, pure verb" "stained
to perfection". Dentate engagement uncalled
for. Drooling bovines deposit the
offal; rediscovering Nature smart poets
nose it. Bottled at source
means just what it says:
Contamination with a designer label.
Elsewhere the oppressed turn shameless:
write them in—they angle
for a cut. Call <u>me</u>
a thief?—"fraudulent" reduces dialectic
to figures. Milk the Lottery
and screw the poor: small
change for beggars means big
bucks in the bush. Here,
bubbles surfacing fast and thick,
extorted sponsorship bloats The Arts.
Which precious semblance replicates self?
Unjustified for the nation, behind
privet, cuttings snipped with the
competitive frillies, fiduciaries chance on
the candytuft Garland*; plotting a
No. 1, the Great Tradition
gets stripped to the skull.
Like patriarchy minus the balls—
enough to make Wendy Cope
forbear. No pearl at the
tip, BUT—same effect, less
sweat—watch out for gush.

On the street a prick
to boot. Vetoed by fax.
Voted a fix. The door-
stepped recipient Pavlovians verify. So
just whose country is this?
Gums clamped on a loose
straw, Freud sucks? Declined for
the Nobel, the superego's at
a discount in a manner
of speaking. Metaphors we die
by. A fox turned tapeworm
did for Persius. Asinine auricles
for purity of diction, extra
terrestrials invade one poet's sleep.
Look at it like them.
Senile, inflated, strictly equal ops.
Ear, less crepitation, cajoled with
maladroit ludic gestures. Disabled access?
Ingredients certified, members are minded.
A seaside postcard chasing the
joke. Off the record, inertia
prescribes imperial measures. Gucci spells
luscious. Minority interests—find one,
get one free. Top Ten?
The Allied Front. Corelli reporting.

* Beatrice Garland: winner of the 2001 National
Poetry Competition.

From the Annals

History records that the Gauls also had their hour of military glory, but since then inaction has sapped their appetite for war. Their valour perished with their freedom.
                            Tacitus

decorated figurehead
a general complying
with textual authority
printed on a pittance
their arms barely
material to a state
the corpus invests

    *

guarded by tongue
"in the name of its god"
a stylistic grace
to credit guesswork
cloudy limits sighted
in the wordage

    *

vide "survey"
"fodder"
under "supervision"
"providential" evidently
invidious

    *

soil rich
in metal proboscis
confronting the riot
shield phalanx

*

the wretched flushed
out
    strategy
against <u>their</u> Nature
crop yield implicit
in rain and mist

*

. . . easier to believe the pearls inferior than that the people turn up their noses at a fat profit.

*

befogged founders
in confusion
new masts
transmit "upright"

*

arithmetic
of our fathers
apostrophes
subtracting
a slave ethos
granite amassed

*

earliest records
in the Book of Memory
as at first light
authority dispenses
summary lessons
from the original
plebeian inflections
to pedagogic decline

*

entered in torn
columns credit
Cogidumnus
landowners
bosses the Party

*

channel dividing
the same ritual
pagani: Joyce
linguistic difference
reduced to a quibble
indistinct across cliff
top villages a perished
liberty *stinks peace*

*

the boot
       fists
You blister
swelling the asphalt's
"piss poor"

*

under title entry
an apron of
abeyance
        montaged for
the Pageant lawn
from moorland verified
in fact ragule
to cadastre two
headed the image
Gaelic levies
a rough total
of napes by default

*

obsolete Shakespearian
shadows of privilege
to be paid for
call it a lottery
that robs us blind

*

a gazetteer of allegiance
tribal disperses through
its line of descent

*

a radical terrain
in eighty
nine volumes
delimiting marches

greenwood and trailer
park kick over
the traces by derivation

      *

   hungry
and wet at the gates
a dejected remnant
bought out
in adverse conditions

      *

impenetrable
forget sylvan's rank
underside
          droplets
retracted
          caterpillar
tracks
tarmac
the penultimate
stammer Not us

Preamble to a Legacy
(after Villon)

Subject (erudite) to post
Millennial light pain   Root
in question essentially verbal
Composed, a good puller
performs from the slot
Dear Reader—vide Barthes
—who says "says PEOPLE"?
the projected plural miscomputes

Date as stated   Cold
snaps a lupine wind-
farmed outcome, beau monde
packed for Mars   Blood
line subject to financial
status, culture grafts take;
leave the blank day
behind, a faraway heartache

New World usage dictates
the first person; upstaged,
thrusters come to grief
Is I otherwise engaged?
Born again venal, underdogs
realise a Nobler Truth:
well endowed's not star
crossed; cupidity inspires belief

in those in favour
Skip the wiles, thanks;
no ascetic or saviour,
pierced belly for flank,
we judge the contents

by the label   Clean
pairs of heels get
ploughed in another field

Sympathy acquits the witch;
victim for the stocks
instead   The braided whip
is metonymic   Re sex:
shape up or ship
out – steerage   The shore
recedes; the suture rips
End of the affair

Out of town, out
of mind   Temperature sub
zero in <u>her</u> heart,
stay, rate, plead, blub
and cut no ice
Distanced, a sinking prick
might sting less than
the St Sebastian kick

Exquisite, her extracted hook
has left its mark
in a fugitive relief;
the bait rejected, gagged,
in rubber, sweated dry
as an Arbroath smoky;
makeshift for a safe
word: Lord have mercy

Filed in your pigeon
hole, there's no appeal:
the sentence is unremitted
Tell the critics syntax

means subjection: their objects
prosper at the till
Potential earnings elsewhere abject,
to itemise my will:

NW1 After-Image

shaky in white caps THE WALLS
OF THE CITY creates its own space
an object lost in urban sprawl
out of focus witness transgresses
the laws of the place brick by brick
to integrate a separation
on the Euston Road the economic
circumscribes some other spring
ghosted her appearance a cameo
in real time the instant of art
a contravention of Planning's veto
memory predicting multiple paths
via nowhere a vision graffitoed
to displace THE TIGERS OF WRATH

Reading Max Jacob

1914

Does lightning have the same shape abroad? Someone at my parents' was discussing the colour of the sky. Is that lightning? A rose-coloured cloud was approaching. How everything changed! God! is it possible for your reality to be so lively? The family home is there; the chestnut trees are glued to the window, the prefecture is glued to the chestnut trees, Mount Frugy is glued to the prefecture: just the peaks, nothing but the peaks! A voice announced "God!" and a brilliant light appeared in the night. An enormous body hid most of the landscape. Was it Him? was it Job? He was wretched, his flesh pierced, his loins concealed by a cloth: what tears, Lord! He was coming down. How? Some larger-than-life couples were coming down too. They were coming through the air in crates, in Easter eggs: they were laughing and the balcony of the family home was littered with powdery black lines. I was afraid. The couples moved into the family home and we watched them through the window. But they were wicked! There were black lines right up to the table cloth and my brothers were picking cartridges apart. Since then I've been under police surveillance.

War

In the night the outer boulevards are deep in snow; the bandits are soldiers; they attack me with guffaws and sabres and empty my pockets: I escape only to fall back into another square. Is it the courtyard of a barracks or an inn? what sabres! what lancers! what snow! I get pricked by a syringe: it's a lethal poison; a death's-head veiled in crepe bites my finger. Hazy streetlamps are spreading the light of my death on the snow.

Declamatory Poem

It is neither the livid awfulness of the sunset nor the sickly dawn that the moon won't illumine, it's the sad light of dreams where you drift capped with sparks, Republics, Defeats, Triumphs! What are these Fates, these Furies? is it France in a Phrygian bonnet? is it you , England? is it Europe? is it the world on the bull-cloud of Minos? There's a great stillness in the air and Napoleon hears the music of silence on the field at Waterloo. O moon, may your horns protect him. A tear runs down his ashen cheeks! the parade of phantoms is so enthralling. "We salute you! our horses' manes are wet with dew, we are the cuirassiers! our helmets shine like stars and in the shadows our dusty battalions are like the hand of Destiny. Napoleon! Napoleon! we are born and we die.—Charge! charge! phantoms! I command you to charge!" The light sneers: the cuirassiers raise their swords in salute and sneer; their flesh and bones are gone. Napoleon hears the music of silence and laments, for where are those forces God gave him? But here comes a drum! It's a child beating a drum: he has a red flag in his bearskin, he has a red flag and that boy is really alive: it is France! It's here now round the field of Waterloo, in the sad light of dreams where you drift capped with sparks, Republics, Defeats, Triumphs, not in the livid awfulness of the sunset, or the sickly dawn that the moon won't illumine.

Poem

I'll erase the heads of the Imperial generals! But they're alive! all I can do is change their hats: the hats are full of gun cotton and these Imperial gentlemen are not joking: the gun cotton lets fly. I didn't know that gun cotton was such a white pigeon. I'll enter this biblical landscape! but it's a wood engraving: an uneven row of houses, a sandy bank behind a stream, a stream behind a palm-tree. It illustrates Saint Matorel, a novel by Max Jacob. Mademoiselle Léonie and I are walking through it, no one warned me you carried suitcases in this novel. The generals seated on that bench were alive, but were Mlle Léonie and I not then? I can't enter this biblical landscape, it's a wood engraving. When the Imperial generals' hats had been restored, everything was in place; I re-entered the wood engraving and peace reigned in the desert of art.

Christmas Story

Once there was an architect or a numskull: more of a numskull than an architect, in Philadelphia, who was instructed: "You know Cologne Cathedral? make one like it!" And, as he didn't know Cologne Cathedral, he was thrown in jail. But in jail an angel appeared to him who said: "Wolfrang! Wolfrang! why be downhearted?" "I have to stay in jail because I don't know Cologne Cathedral!" "You need a Rhine wine to build Cologne Cathedral, but let them see the plan and you'll get out of jail." And the angel gave him the plan, and he showed them the plan and got out of jail, but he could never build the cathedral because he couldn't find the Rhine wine. He had the idea of importing Rhine wine to Philadelphia, but they sent him a frightful French Moselle, so he couldn't build Cologne Cathedral in Philadelphia: he could only manage a frightful Protestant chapel.

Cubism and Sun Diluted

L'ecclesiglia del Amore, l'odore del Tarquino, in short, all the monuments of Rome on a *bottleglia* of wine and the corresponding account to confirm you've had a good drink, but you'll be abstaining in future: the bottleneck of the bowl and the tetotaller's tap. If you have to repent it, you might just as well abstain. The unstable rainbow is only a volcanic motif in the luggage tag's corner. Motus! and let's compare litres: *el spatio del Baccio* and the *Bacco nel cor*.

Literary Manners

When two groups of men of letters meet, it is rare for the greetings not to be accompanied by smiles. When a group of them meets a man of letters on his own, if there is an initial hearty greeting, the greetings diminish, till sometimes the last of the group doesn't bother at all. It seems I wrote that you had bitten a woman's nipple till it bled. If you believe I did it why do you offer me greetings? and, if I believe you did it, why do I greet you? We met at the house of an imposing woman with glasses and a knitted shawl, you shook my hand, but we found ourselves in the room with the woman's commode and you threw the commode's seat-cushions at my head. These cushions were very 18th century. The word is that I threw some cushions at you too rather than try to justify myself. I don't know if that's true. When my group meets you, if I'm the last and don't greet you, don't think it's because of the cushions episode; but if our groups meet and smiles should be exchanged, don't think mine's among them.

Journeys

I'll never get out of here: I hurry to say goodbye to my aunt, I find the family in lamplight; they offer me endless advice, my bag is packed, but my suit is still at the cleaner's, I arrive at the cleaner's: I hardly recognise my suit: it's not mine, it's been switched for another! no, that's the one, but horrendously stretched, disfigured, torn, restitched, edged with black. Outside two lovely Breton girls are laughing beside a linen trolley: no time to follow them; bah! at night they'll be going the same way as me. I notice the street names have changed; Lorient now has a "Power of the Lyric" street. What astonishing council advice to make the night give streets names like that. At the hotel, it occurs to me to check the cleaner's receipt: 325 francs, free delivery. Am I going mad? The café is all eyes, I meet a painter from Paris! I have trouble shaking off. He's all over me here, even though we nettled one another before: I'm so late I skip the handshake—and no cab! While one's being found, some childhood friends plead with me to stop off at Le Mans! not at Le Mans, at Nogent! not at Nogent, because we're on bad terms with the ... oh! God! I'm losing the plot completely ... I end up welshing on an I.O.U. to a piano remover. And the dry-cleaner? Here I am in a weird, but very distinguished outfit: this grey frock coat, too bulky owing to the excess of underwear I have on to lighten my bag! This formal top hat, what travelling clothes. Oh! I've forgotten to say goodbye to ... And the dry-cleaner! I've missed the train, the only train: tomorrow I'll have to start all over again! The thought of it won't let me get to sleep.

1889-1916

In 1889, the trenches were laid in wax and put under glass. Two thousand meters under ground, two thousand shackled Poles didn't know what they were doing there: the nearby French discovered an Egyptian buckler: it was shown to the world's greatest doctor, the one who had pioneered the ovariotomy. The world's greatest tenor sang two thousand notes in the theatre that measures two thousand meters round: he made two million and gave them to the Institut Pasteur. The French were under glass.

In the Silent Forest

Night has not yet come to the silent forest and the thunderstorm of sadness has not yet damaged the leaves. To the silent forest the Dryads have fled, the Dryads will not return.

In the silent forest the stream has no ripples because its ebbing waters have run low.

In the silent forest there is a tree as black as black and behind the tree there is a bush shaped like a head in flames, aflame with flames of blood and gold.

In the silent forest to which the Dryads will not return, there are three black horses, they are the three horses of the Magi and the Magi are no longer on their horses or anywhere else to be found and their horses are talking like men.

Kaleidoscope

Everything was as in a mosaic: the animals were walking with their feet in the air except for the donkey whose white belly was inscribed with words that kept changing. The tower was an opera glass; there were gilded tapestries with black cows; and as for the little princess in a black gown, you couldn't be sure if the gown was patterned with green suns or if you were seeing her through holes in the material.

We Saw It But It's Impossible

It's a very small town but it's by a river; saying river I mean "embankment". On this embankment—a wilderness—there's a small hotel that belonged to a widow: one modest storey and some attic rooms with wrought iron balconies. It was turned into a public library without books. I came there to work in the evenings on a wide worn table that had been painted black. One evening the attendant told me: "There's something new up there!" There was something new: several figures from the Revolution were sat round my table. Mirabeau was not as ugly as they say he was: he has a youthful neck and all his body's force is concentrated in his mouth; Vergniaud had . . . I'll not describe my stupefaction! —On the second floor I found Diderot on a mantelpiece, very much reduced in size. He was naked under a dressing-gown and was discussing the *Mercure de France* with Mme Rachilde. No-one wanted to believe in my ghosts. The next day I returned with a friend whom I presented to the shades. The day after that he didn't want to admit their reality, despite having been properly introduced.

For M. Modigliani to Show Him I Am a Poet

The cloud is the inter-continental mail
Exile's syllabary that sentenced by Hell
To wrestle themselves in floods of tears
The oceans won't spell out in their glassy sphere.
The black mountain peaks nod off on their terrace
Furrows God ploughed to hide the race of man
Not reading the secret in the passing cloud
He doesn't know what is in his hand
But when his enemy the wind gives chase
He turns roaring and hurls a foot of brass.
I was a gifted child. Waking, the sky's mass
Of reflections carried over the spells
From my dreams till reality's colours were eclipsed.
In the midst of friends, schooled by angels
I knew not who I was and I wrote a bit.
One day I met God instead of a woman
The companion who embroiders my being
Without my even knowing him
He is peace and gaiety
He's the root of security
And to celebrate his mysteries
He's made me his secretary
Now through the nights I decipher
The figures-covered sheet of paper
He penned in his own hand
And posted to my mind.
In the aquarium of the air there lurk indiscreet
Demons breaking the cloud up to steal its secret.

Villonelle

Tell me what was the song
The lovely sirens sang
That made the Greeks ship oars
And lean out from the bows.

Achilles who defeated Troy
In a horse crammed with sounds
Achilles was no whipping boy
But, he was captured by the songs
The Hellenic virgins sang
Tell me, Venus, I pray
What was their melody

A prisoner in Tripoli
Composed one in his cell
So sweet they set him free
Restored him to his family
That had wept beneath the walls

Nausicaa at the fountain
Penelope weaving wool
Zeuxis at work on a panel
Were singing the fol-de-rol! . . .
And what were the songs of the swains?

Echoes of the wide plains'
Echoes and the migrants' songs!
Where are the old refrains
That we sang again and again,
The girls who seemed divine
As they snared love with a song?
And can I remember mine?

Madame X

So exotic the swish
Of your hips,
        So daft
Your basque's embrace,
        Near naked
So scanty your lace,
That if your headdress
        Doesn't say yes
Nothing below
        The brow's said no.

Cemetery

If you drive my sailor out
you will send him to his grave,
white rose, roses white and red.

My grave is like a garden,
like a garden white and red.

On Sunday you will go, white rose,
promenading with the rest,
white rose and lily white,

at All Saints' Aunt Yvonne
brings a wreath of painted iron
out of her cottage garden
painted iron with pearls of satin,
red rose and lily white.

If God wishes me to go
to Heaven I shall climb, white rose,
crowned with a golden halo,
white rose and lily white.

If my sailor should return,
red rose and rose white,
to my graveside he would come,
white rose and lily white.

Don't forget when we were young, white rose,
when we played along the quays,
white rose and lily white.

The Acrobat in Third Class

The acrobat! the acrobat
caught the express at 9.30 flat
took the Paris-Nantes express
Hurry up, hurry my acrobat
it's not a train you'd want to miss
And here's the song that sings in her heart:
oh! to follow through the balmy night
the course of a river winding from sight
through the western night, the widowed night!
But they don't want to leave me be
deep in my dream with my willow tree
Saumur! Saumur! you of Saumur
leave me like salted meat to cure. *
Saumurians, please avoid this car.
She's dreaming of her lyotard
that has to match her golden hair
when it streams behind her through the air
She dreams of her husband who is young
younger than she, and of her son
a veritable prodigy.
The acrobat is a Circassian
She's bang on time when she beats the big drum
She has beauty and no braggadocio
she has lips just like a tomato.

---

* Saumur is on the line to Nantes; a *saumure* is a pickle.

Do You Know Meister Eckhart?

Paul Petit.

Do you know Albert the Great?
Joachim? Amaury de Bène?
Margareta Ebner the Thössian
with child by Christ incarnate?

Do you know Henri Suso?
Ruysbrock dubbed the Admirable?
Joseph de Cupertino
who flew like a dirigible?

And the sermons of Jean Tauler?
and the Seven Sisters' little man
looked after like an Amazon
when he landed from the ether?

Do you know Jacob Boehm
and his Signatura Rerum?
Paracelsus' Archidoxis
the X-ray test's prognosis?

We barely know those we esteem
but I understand them well enough
all those of whom I'm one
and not a whit less a baboon.

Wars and America

Your turn, American anthill! Put on your nurses' and officers' uniforms! Hotels became fantastic bureaus. What activity in the lifts and at reception! One fine day, it was like the thunder's nail-scratch on a cloud: the cashier's figures were out by millions; many committed suicide; many went mad; crowded lifts stopped between floors and couldn't be restarted. People's spirits still bubbled with optimism wonderfully, but it was increasingly only verbiage and farmyard clucks. The bright idea of a change of direction came up: but no! each new leader confronted fresh lies, a jungle of delusions.

Love of One's Neighbour

Who saw the toad cross the street? it's an homunculus: a doll couldn't be smaller. He's crawling on his knees; would you say he's a penitent? No! he has rheumatism, one leg lags behind and he drags it along! where's he going like that? he's out of the sewer, poor clown. No-one noticed this toad in the street. There was a time when no-one noticed me in the street, now the children jeer at my yellow star. Lucky toad not to have one!

Eurochants

I

1

    fogged cave; hours tenebrous
    A Camden Town alba
                        preterition's rainbow bands
    lent selflessly to pacify letters
    The courtesies soul observes
                            song a moiled vein
    Monkish desire for paupered spirit
                                  speech prints
    two voices a phantom tongued
                          annotation
    unintended, Guglielmi: le double pouvoir
    or, selenic revery astray: l'océan des Spectres
    en danse, privation an attractive taint;
    the readerly asleep to facts
    Rendition then a quittance;
    jet trail before Luna; indeterminate
    a kiss before dying

2

redbrick rubric register slip
incipit the mix close
up
    face cut into
two presents overlap
                      lip
at the nipples' rejected
image
        remorae in memoriam
who's feelings?
            sutra stitched
(congrès buccal) (système fleuve)
i lumi bei gathered from the drift
exterior filmic eros secretes
gone beyond what land is this?
appearance the same being oblivious

3

"... bien loin de toi! trop tard! jamais Peut-être! ..."
  Charles Baudelaire

  for Sean Bonney

trilobée triangulates
a public space
             traffic hurlait
its liminal channel's street
talk drowned
             in black ink
grief's fugitive run down
                         de
iced
    zwei Finger in dir;
crushed velvet diachronous
oneiric minglings
                 ciel livide
bas de sa vulve

            sorE
looking back Ô toi gap
fond measure of irrelation
a moot absence distances
the nothing beauty tongued

4

neonomian in transit
(primo corpo poi mente)
a precipitate plenitude's
monotone congruence
Amaryllis Tiefimschnee
Traced north from thaw myth
Siegfried vergisst
White-out to lead white
ecru crusted twigs
frissons d'ombelles a scattering
regathered doxa from allegory
"demons and outsiders"
staccato da tutto
                  "écrire sans voyelles"
Date and place age sex
register submitted subject to correction
the body extrapolates a former nowhere
in the continuity of events

l'Oméga zeroed in
Dein Gesang, was weiß er?
A cosmic synthesis Hebraic interrupts
silk-needled from an angle
pulse and breath rising
out of its silence
                  rois blancs
under the banners
a fresh breeze
echoes
for the proverbial white page

5

> "*Comme Hécaté tu me feras errer …*"
> Maurice Scève

which witch definitive erratic shades
the dead-and-alive silence
                    verdict:
a hypothetical deux mille années
absence presenting a deep split
dans le verbe made flesh Délie stripped
poilus in silk shift to the couch
ardour vacated hot-foot to a figment
head united with moons and tide

blood relative to a future shelved
being possessed where *is* this?
in black and white the injunction: change
or else thrown out from the centre
former haunts vain thoughts
                            a half of us
suburban planes resolve at the margin

6

Tel un mirage triste l'autre s'eloigne, se reporte à l'infini
 Roland Barthes

    episodic in perspective
    breasts orbiting
    periodically pearls un
    strung *mythoplokon* go
    between on la guette
    entre
    le français et
    l'italien il tuo pallido
    Viso superimposed
    stopgap Picasso: Jeune
    femme en chemise
    1905
    plus d'image
    for a timeless moment
    le bleu délavé
    of her jeans rien
    que du langage
    ones and zeros
    a vertical column
    withdrawn from the wound
    an entrance regressing
    all the way handprints
    behind the words
    what was it speaking?
    a nameless exemplar
    tra le statue embodied
    immutably Ella m'appar
    liquidée

7

> "*War ich je hier?*"
> Ingeborg Bachmann, *Abschied von England*

stepped on a land
stone disturbed
drips oak
-leaved distances mist
their sylvan metropolis
air and angles
a legendary credit
from high rise
to razed tracks
at its words' edge
the quest meaning
plain blocks
gulls flap between
ectoplasmic traffic
a grey
-green trade
-in
    imperial measures
emptied for landfill
naturally
ungesagt
damp flags
the god
-given
presumptive borders

8

> *"Domna, pois de mi no.us chal…"*
> Bertrans de Born

hegemonic Other tongues twisted
outline for gist—Deleuze
A presence grasped at
                egal
no.us posc trobar
Particle to ephemera
shades, mirror
-image
        recto a total body so-called
Autumn drapes synecdoche or fetish
Cerulean framed villas
chestnut dross
De chascuna un bel:
index Anhes / Jeanne
Substitute Ideal wisps édit
Epidermis occult
eclipsed blue network

"frontier or fissure?" transgresses interface velvet creased
Bathed in un mot doux
moon
its damp basement mucus sheathes
Soisseubuda
ou
visages coulés
                Curtains
Parted sur le même
moule declensions' flushed
inverse
        le plan de vos hanches
Erased

9

"... vide una donna che riceve honore ..."
                    Dante

sidereal drifter
        extra
cosmic suspirations
thick and fast launch
pad to figment
        in dream
evoked free
fall une femme
        Botticelli
de visage
    vulval
an inversive Eros
zeroed on desire
peregrino misaddressed
nella qualità di costei
optative
    a word
web of innerness
its designation: ONE WAY
Incarnated
        ethereal
a fugitive at face
value
   before
defunctive reunion
aime criaient-ils

10

> "… *mas amors mi asauta* …"
> Arnaut Daniel

influence Provençal avenues' petrol haze
yielding its series
l'Avril de mon age liberates
NUIT VERTE OU ROUGE

urban plane
poster trail some other spring licks

a labial ci git
inscriptive cleft

silk-lined lame metonym
in wishful fixation

a *where am I?* declined brought to book

11

> *"Sarai tu ... "*
> Cesare Pavese

blue skies thinking "nomadic"
sunyata an odour of stone
quell vuoto lontano
tra le case objectified
nothing; analogue
migrant
      from its borders to re
write the tribe al centro del mondo

where are you? in the indifference
di borgate tristi, beduine
streets delivered of old hurts
Heimkunft for la scavatrice

comptant les jours
in doorways' caves
le scandal du silence
                graffiti erase
la main de l'ombre
qui
vous prend

Retornos del amor
in faceless crowds
           one last
telepathic plea and
lost to sight tourner
douloureusement
le coin
    a damaged case
abandoned at ARRIVALS

II

1

    night and day demi brume
    Centrepoint; "La Chanson ..."
                                   an untexted legacy
    its realization
             image décolleté;
    separation for flesh qui sèche, jaunit;
    le désir a trace toujours absent
                         reference back
    Dante: che troppo mi piacesse
                          a tongue
    erased in plurivocal harangue
    Tape loop with psychic hiss
                      a stream
    mephitic jetsam
                l'androgyne under neon;
    ascesis and freak-out from the upper
    deck
        acts for simulacra
    Tottenham Court Road: masonry
    signposts a discontinued route

2

La voix black
and white after
image d'
une autre année
the ideal
doubles
      oltre tutti i divisori
a faded outline
          delle epoche
carnally all there
shaped by the New Thing
global designates a non
occurrence outcast
in the Zone nerve
ends register who
is she? in close
up phantasmal
body to abstract
background music

3

"*Un éclair ... puis la nuit!* ... "
    Charles Baudelaire

  for Sean Bonney again

Longue mince
a storm germ damps
son œil lids veil
hem cropped in black
a SHOCK from skirt
FLASH fleshed scales climb
sa jambe peeping
lusts nape to bust
crisped in the next seat
not to know Ô
toi whose the wish
qui tue a glimpse
imped on lack far
off intense

4

> *"Die bleiben und winken, wissen es nicht."*
> Paul Celan

quai de départ
dark moist clinging
clothes scuffed a suitcase
of cash empty trucks
back on Bahnsteig
Zwei currency restricted
business dealt lots
thistles measure embankments
collapsing trunks blurred
with the word for home

Wegrander goods yards
subsistence from stone
obol tongued shadow
poppies bridge
               displaced
a transient caress
networks Tsvetayeva
Augärten Marchfeld
slipped through the grids
injuries recede to
the point zeros replicate

sleeping car intertexts
a poor exchange tracks
abstractive memory confused
survival lines crossing
dreamless deletes lovers
location ás fable
beyónd the arc
lights objectively lost

5

Vien da veduta a phantasmal
other inscribed THE END
City Road / Greek Street one
way signs reverse creaturely
turned to images fading
shades in the misty light of Mars

(pas de ville / cité sans itération)
gemination for mythic progress;
fleshed essence beyond cathexis
woman / city reproductive frames

reference back: displaced matrix;
forma futuri a virtual Eve;
oltre di natura eroticised
streetscapes' slabs echo nothing declared

6

drafts   edits
a question of context
d'horizon repeated
vertical Greek border
at 90° the face
colours unpredictably
exodus for red flags'
heritage culture
se torsifler la lingua transplanted
a succession of bent notes
jouée et rejouée
between sky and air
a superficial difference
spelled out to grieve ón
the image collapsed into urban facts

mamelons du parc
body / art / language
in usum Delphini
the number 3
shaft   bush
arched by design
fountains from hidden depths
established brands spray
canned
anthropomorphic
hands yield to tags
parts written in the target mix:
miscegenation
bricolage
stretto
subject verging on an abstract state
Pythagorean
a touch overblown

7

> *"J'ai quitté mon pays …"*
> Ali Farka Touré

smoke screens abut no fixed diaspora
metaphoric a Kafka affect adieu Savane
fault in the joints split press
ganged aspens tremble assent métisse
employed a bridge meaning sense
J'ai trouvé le métro
trafficked between cultures un porto
disperato the faceless response
native tabac frustrates
a choice of tranche mother
tongue encoded fetish
l'image du mot dans mot
TATTOO transliterates keel
scraped knuckles nominative
abstracts' un petit boulot
for station doorway raw
skinned statistics under
the clock historic parole refashioned

8

    "La piaga, ch'io credea che fosse salda …"
           Gaspara Stampa

La piaga intermittent
si desta residual
voci e risvegli à l'heure où
je vous revois pale and faint
en fouillant parmi les livres
Philoctetes indexical
                 blood
and puss jusqu'au mot: primavera
phantomic
         attended
Risponderai
         Les mots réels
fioriranno dans ton corps

no space for novi lacci self
interfering patterns at the neck
parole antiche more or less
unlooseable knots
               loco
for motive
       a figment's attesting
martyr
     unaccepted
terminal letters the true voice
of feeling dumped

9

"… echéronse a sus pies los serafines …"
            Pedro Espinosa

                    for Will Rowe

nubes y celajes
            lymphatic modified
Milky Way
            nymphal stop
-gap impervious exploratory
                        candle
-power targets blank

                episode lexical
Airy residue
            Symbolist carpets' knots cup sap
-lisping plated lily

                gas globes'
melting odalisque parergon
-strapped
        aspirant baggage
                    ARRIVALS
paged
    inciensos multiplies
ectopic trajectories uncoupling sun
and moon

            lift in ascent
                    voyeur
-pressure raised

                            what else?

"outside" the Word to boot-lick

10

lettered METAPHORIKI
(Hocquard) a quay
side truck Cargoed
d'oblio Passing Ships
upper limit 11
/69 gold chain
ed to a fixed star
its space shrunk
referent: cette voile
alternative sequential
shrouds
        a clean sheet
usati segni his own
er inked the same
the frame changes
flotsam pro tem was
hed up recurrently from
old hurts to harbour
Loyalty and Art
misplaced

11

> *Je pars plus amoureux que je ne fus jamais*
> Racine, *Bérénice*

corporate dreams her figure
liquidates A populace flows
Thru
    this dialogue of one
a basement perspective
Agar Grove rent owed
entropic decades;
in the balance:
cero rebosante;
le petit bunker du sexe
transcendent
          moonset
with throbbings
              les tombes des astres

cento for synthesis
les lèvres dependent
on nomi indecifrabili:
their faces blurred through
salive di spettri instants
link back
      poca eco
from its hollow throat
a life versed in your loss
what survives love shelved

III

1

sea mist
        Ulysse—dilapidate
the landing stage
              le sûtra
de Non-Retour
                  urban pool
for foreign soil
            tutta sua dolcezza
carried over qui cesse de clignoter
Blurred clusters distant
                      beyond the Thames
a summer night's reverse
-image screened
                some other time
In vocative shutdown to another tune
la sua loquela n'ont pas su
répondre: untraced / epitaphic;
not altering by one iota
the things love keeps us from

2

    drafts and fragments traced
back
        from merveilleuses bribes
the imperfect (bis)
                where were we
together in spirit the words
yours le trou dans le lan
gage
        aperture; negative
                    window
beyond lamp in cyclic orientation;
te possideant aliae mapping
otherwise
        Del cors li fos
Gestalt in analog deficit
futurity roofless
            studio
to devastate "Son Dezirat"
erased the subject
            2nd person
lost in the etymon;
delay a song dissolving

3

one more for Sean

scrambled solvents crushed lusts
Crowd to spat brick
streets skirt catastrophe
flesh itch lines tongue
Black piss night fugitive;
lip hooked Ô toi split
time triangulates a wish
talk drowned
              my face
a public space traffics
Love at first sight
griefs froze
              stigmata'd instant;
gaze bewitched
              livid
pitiless veiled farewells

4

> *Setz deine Fahne auf Halbmast*
> Paul Celan

documentary ephemera
                    rubble preludes
peripheral
        origins skipped: Madrid
press flash diminished Zwillingsröte
ballot box slow roads
to this creed arch
geographic
        planet in shorthand
los dos se desnudaron
EIN BLATT at half
mast being flesh dematerialized
means the same rounding
love ignorance repeated
                    exodus
to shibboleth persons against
nature statistics slaughtered in
a red black roar

5

a two blue between
suburbs' and shadows' ominous
cul de sac the voice
doubles in vertical exit
a scentless presence true
to herself elsewhere
starts here instinct
hypostatic backdrop redbrick
weatherboard aspirants' "I"
on license rôle for myth
cloned at street level
third person globalised
but for her the message
"j'ai perdu" figments
network the derelict centre

6

                    clustereded asters
Outside below balustrade differences
exclude displace in this one
Night mists brightly
                    Classed the present
phenomena wilt
                  lit room eyeline
stripped on review
Iron rim engravings illustrate
suited Bruxelles tulips
                    Gravel crunching
history in reverse moons
images fixes ou morcellement
de l'espace
          Interface:
wet-leaf-pasted window pane
visibly left
            the shoulder hidden
Occult sources proscribe Magritte
Beast impressed tips brush
her nipple's image the mirrors double
Mamelons ample
                balusters impel
Platonic distance
                Heraclitus equally
a potential reflection
                Head over
      Heels in
Rivers "as ever"

7

> *Detrás del horizonte abierto*
> Vicente Huidobro, 'El otro puerto'

the same for place
Estrellas eléctricas
in metonymic chains
sparks in the wind
drift snuffed habitat
to zone a narrative
of proper names border
posts orphaned a market
in transit peasant thirsts
shelter suspended
on a higher plane
whole for its parts
zodiacal figured
economy das Heim
                    des émigrants the song
at mobile numbers'
ports of call
a tongue unspoken

8

> *Je m'apparus en toi comme une ombre lointaine*
> Mallarmé

parole in reverse
script left to rot
moist lips
mist mirror
split traumatic
scrolled flesh
a catalogue
des feuilles
sous ta glace
vacancy refracts
faint scars'
peeled backing
epidermal trapped

9

        breathless
aetherial luft
von anderen planeten
cataractic planched
al cor dolente
olfactory deficit
un odore di vento
in astral residues'
pedestrian drift
Fatally inflated
Vegliai le stele
per il tuo divenir

eternal declines
"suck"
    head
to feet erratic malodorous;
no return on lunar
oppressive coupling
               und du
Geliebter schatten
aspirationally grounded
inhuman cycles
love your face

10

> *Et tu a couru vers lui …*
> Jacques Prévert

raincoat belted
sous la pluie its
errant address
narrative dates
a paratactic impulse
sans cesse ces bri
bes ce format the flesh
sweats ink washed
to a misty dissolve
she had left before
memory's embrace
ghosted City Road
Fuor di cholore
a preterite's flickering
animus redeemed
visage heureux
figurative
essere diviso
an elsewhere the limp
id self
image filmed

11

> "*Je me souviens pour être malheureux/heureux—
> non pour comprendre.*"
>   Roland Barthes: *Fragments d'un discours amoureux*

L'histoire bourré de thèmes
remade in the act bouquet
sur l'échafaud a play
versed in your loss
rendered between tenses
endless becoming an end
in itself l'imparfait
murmure derrière ce présent
s'aprirà una porta
utterance for iter
rating anachronous her figure
liquidates a serial ab
sence Charing Cross Road
Bastille Piazza di Spagna
the chronic image traced in spl
it ink a vagabond ob
session Ce théâtre
du temps: tu rientrerai
le leurre de la mémoire
E lucevan le stelle
from an unlovely street
EXIT to the overture
too late to perform
the last draft of her script
reads "Our children"

Terminal Preludes

… L'homme a lâché les fins du monde
qu'il conservait depuis mille ans
au fond d'un coeur peuplé d'orties.
Il ne nous reste qu'a nous taire
et contempler ce jeune atome
qui a raison de la montagne,
cet océan qui ce suicide …

homage to Alain Bosquet

aerial zones gated
report back from lacteal;
reptilian stone a market loader
declensions emit fixed

say NO
to cargo
disaster
plasmatic futures' crisped surplus;
in the hot news
roadblocked pores ópen galactic intercourse

corrective:
spores
spheres;
discord incongruous:
émigré simples' violative therapy

"ideologue"
"racinate"
predictive shards;
grids guárd a gyratory nothing

        boulevard scene
        -stealers
              spectacle theorized
        seasonal mirage
        a corroded bust

        Modernity off
        -screen
              spent dreams
insurgent graveyards maximize
    monumental percentages
necessity's granite loss leader figureheads
        obliged to depart

        seditious tracks
     flesh the intersection
     Ducasse triangulates
        rue du Bac
         Nadja
         object
  to abject desired absence

  Quand la ville se soulève
underground rendered a last corner
      negative markers
      deny Mallarmé
    the city's blank page

millennium general intention protective
painless interstates
temples pre-stressed;
horizon scans computed
suspect divination
guerrillas framed

proportionality contingent
requisitive
suits pronounced opposing
troops conclude

cunt-lack upgrade
graduate lapse;
lip synch evidence demotic
encrypted
90 miles distant
dead on time

telltale on the water-table
rain nails the estimate's base

serendipitous subject to agency
last cars in algebraic scribbles:
a pervasive ROAD CLOSED to dope out the odds

footprints linger convincing science
gauged inches cancel

hydropic:
invasive;
surveyal:
aorist:
a series of graphs depression levelled

backspill passsage to abeyant matrix;
gas station forecourts
scattered in puddles at either side

le mot amorphous;
allotments' late frost

tendrils channel hereon in nothing

sintatticamente contracted
co-ordinates nipt
anticipate groundswell from scuttled alba
refloat the page soft wet vocables lap

lexicon at your service
elsewhere reverse
"absorb desert setback"
tribal orbits dwindled in the loop

azure freight;
naufrage du ciel;
airwaves' growth
-enabled oceanologic lapse

post-catastrophe
acqueous profit;
relict:
le luci's increment expelled

north score;
thaw myths

un petit coin de néant;
monotony
a denial

beast coast bruised flat
EXXON locates traffic labyrinths
in lurid mist

orbital
starlit
sluggish on nymphal drift
horizons obsess a viscous fetish;
le mépris
de l'espace
exacted
a ghastly aesthetic
framed in black

red gesture;
ratio agent strait fleshed
snakeskin continua eliminate the concept

illusional accentuates
nacre
cleat
epact;
nude code
root words
blood
-draped agapist
a zoom blurs petals ethos severs

epiphanic frame;
apocalypse
scaled spasm

rigour traced
disesteem forbids
esoterica
to exorcised asteroid squeeze

fuel crop to carbon sink in circuit burn-out
instinct processing little intimacy
the time-lapse forbidden
virus miniaturised
lives dependent on abiding night

Mosaic chronology to eliminate:
Quattrocento handprint in Platonic trajectory
through too much space;
natural satellite
planetic spillout
a phallic passage to erase the gap

blind urge linear module
accelerate feedback unembodied;
amnesiac encomia
monument to impact:
no deal on the mists of no return

www.ingramcontent.com/pod-product-compliance
Lightning Source LLC
Chambersburg PA
CBHW031158160426
43193CB00008B/418